The Book
of
MAN
LAW

Volume 1

CHARLES E. CASTEEL JR.

The Book of Man Law

Charles E. Casteel Jr.

ISBN (Print Edition): 979-8-64247-6826

ISBN (eBook Edition): 978-1-54396-046-4

TABLE OF CONTENTS

Acknowledgments

The completion of this book could not have been possible with-out the love, help and support of so many. I would like to spotlight a few.

First, I would like to thank my dear mother, Gloria S. Casteel for giving me life and providing the ultimate example of womanhood. She is truly the best mother a guy can have.

I would like to thank the many direct and indirect contributors to this book. Special thanks to my father/hero/friend/fraternity brother/mentor, Charles E. Casteel Sr, the greatest son a father can have, Charles E. Casteel III, and my incredible little brother/friend/ expert sports analyst, Kevin L. Casteel, who provided the inspiration and editorial support for the publication of this manuscript.

I would also like to thank David E. Phillips, Author of The Success Pyramid, and a true friend for the advice and support he provided toward my work.

Thanks to my fellow "Knights of the Roundtable" – Stephan Deville, Chuck Smith, Mike Thigpen and Wayne Tucker – my best friends for the past 30+ years. We have laughed together, shed a man-tear or two, and had each other's back since we were teenagers. They are my brothers for life.

I would also like to thank and recognize the brothers of Omega Psi Phi Fraternity Incorporated, especially our most noble deceased founders – Dr. Ernest E. Just, Professor Frank Coleman, Dr. Oscar J. Cooper and Bishop Edgar A. Love, along with the brothers of Gamma Pi Chapter - Prince George's County, Maryland. Omega was established under the principles of Manhood, Scholarship, Perseverance, Uplift and has been an extraordinary part of my life since birth. Indeed, 'Friendship is Essential to the Soul.'

Finally, and most importantly, I would like to thank my loving and supportive wife, Renee. She provided the inspiration and motivation for me to move this project forward. I am tremendously blessed and grateful to have her. Marrying her was the best decision I ever made.

Introduction

One Sunday evening, in the Fall of 2018, I was literally sitting   at a hotel bar in downtown Tampa, Florida with my brother Kevin and oldest son Charles III (Tre') celebrating the Washington Redskins 16-3 win over the Tampa Bay Buccaneers, when the idea for this book materialized.

As part of an annual tradition, my father (Charles Sr.), Kevin, Tre' and I wait anxiously for the NFL schedule to come out. We then choose one road-game to attend to watch our favorite football team (the Washington Redskins) play. This year we decided to visit Tampa.

Being that both my parents were born and raised in Tampa, and we still had plenty of family in the area, it was the perfect opportunity to knock out a few birds with one stone. We got to visit with family from both sides, eat some of our favorite southern foods and see our team win on the road. It was an awesome trip! But win or lose, the annual fellowship with my father, brother and son is beyond price-less. This is male bonding at its best.

Now, back to the bar. My father had already turned-in for the evening. Therefore, the three of us were downstairs watching Sunday Night football, when the topic of Man Law violations was introduced. While enjoying victory drinks, we shared stories of recent violators we had all encountered. The conversation took off. Even the bartender began chiming-in, and we laughed and laughed for over an hour. Then it hit me. We are in the throes of an epidemic. Grown men are wearing skinny jeans for god sakes! Something must be done. I will step-up to the task. I will write a book.

The Book of Man Law is intended to provide a humorous yet realistic perspective on how men are to govern themselves in general. Until recently, these laws have been mostly un-published but widely known and practiced by generations of men world-wide.

Due to the sudden rise of overt Man Law violations, the author felt it was both timely and necessary to develop a formal manuscript to help set the record straight.

Although this book has been written and published, under no circumstances should anyone be approached, reprimanded, assaulted nor physically or verbally abused as a result of this publication or any perceived violations. The purpose of this book is to entertain, educate and help stem-the-tide of Man Law violations. It is meant to be a quick reference guide and has been divided into sections for ease of use. Ultimately, we as men need to police ourselves and act accordingly. Together we can make a difference.

In the beginning, on the sixth-day, God created Adam…and Man Law was born.

What is Man Law?

Laws that ALL MEN must abide by. All Man Law orig-inates once declared or laid down by ONE MAN then agreed to by MANY. It is then said to be 'law.'

Who is Governed by Man Law?

ALL MEN! However, grace may be extended to those under the age of 10. Everyone else should know better.

The Basics
Articles 1-29

1. Never shake another man's hand while sitting down, unless both parties are seated or he is extremely vertically challenged. Shaking hands sitting down would mean you are in a lower position than the man you are shaking hands with. Females are supposed to offer their hand to a guy without standing. Men should always stand up to shake hands

2. Always give a firm/strong right-handed hand shake ONLY with eye contact. No squinting or fast blinking allowed during the process…unless the meeting is taking place during a wind storm or other extreme weather event

3. The official order of the three S's is: Shit – Shower – Shave. However, they are somewhat interchangeable, but the 'SHI' should never follow the 'SHO'

4. Respect your elders ALWAYS. Some may smell a little funny, but just ignore it

5. Seniority rules. Neophytes are expected to make all food/alcohol runs, help with setup and cleanup, ride in the backseat, take out the trash, etc. Age has its benefits

6. The proper way to hug another man (other than documented family members) is hand shake with right hand, while reaching around with left hand (maximum 2 pats on the back) above the shoulder blades only. No pole-to-pole contact. 3-seconds max

7. The proper way to hug another man's woman: Respectful church hugs only. Adhere to the 3-second rule referenced in article 6. If she is clearly out of his league, you may have an additional 1.5 seconds of hug time

8. Eye contact with another man's woman must be limited to 2.5 second increments. Again, extra time may be allotted based on article 7

9. Never wish another man 'Happy Birthday' via phone call or text before 9:00 am. Failure to adhere will send the wrong message, as if you were waiting with bated breath anticipating the arrival of his special day

10. If you ever get introduced to your ex's new man, it is mandatory that you squeeze the hell out of his hand, especially if he is taller, better looking or makes more money than you

11. When walking by another man in tight spaces, when contact is possible, it is only acceptable to proceed by passing through back-to-back (AKA hole to hole) or face-to-face (AKA pole to pole) without eye contact

12. When attending a seated event with another man, always adhere to the buffer rule: man, empty chair, man. If all other seats are taken, you may proceed with sitting side by side

13. If you hold hands with another man
(i.e. joining hands in prayer), your
fingers MUST never interlock. That's
just wrong. You must also avoid arm
swinging and unnecessary finger
movement throughout the process

14. If attending a seated event with another couple (with the seats all in a row), the seating arrangement should be as follows: man, woman, woman, man

15. Never dance one on one or too close to another man. For the love of God, DO NOT VIOLATE this Man Law

16. Man tears: Absolutely no crying in public. The only exceptions include – loss of family member or close friend; your dog dies; your team loses on the final play of the championship game, or your team wins the championship after a long unfair hiatus

17. When another man offers you gum or breath mint, take it – no questions asked. Take the hint

18. Never ask another man to scratch your back. The most he can do in dire circumstances is give you a hard slap

19. Never rub anything on another grown
man; i.e. suntan lotion; ointment; etc.
Must we say more? I didn't think so

20. When invited to another man's house, ALWAYS ask to bring something. If the answer is 'no', bring something anyway. They will talk about you if you don't

21. Whatever you take to the party stays at the party even if it wasn't opened. It may hurt a little and you might shed a man-tear for leaving an expensive unopened bottle behind, but it is the right thing to do

22. No man should ever text a smiley
    face to another grown man. Just don't

23. When joking another man, the ONLY thing off limits is his children. Everything else, especially his appearance, is fair game. Conduct yourselves accordingly

24. No holiday or birthday gift exchanges between grown men outside of family. The only exception is 'gag gifts' for significant milestones. Your wife and kids have controlling interest over your wallet as it is

25. Don't be the 'old man at the club'. Look around. If you discover that you are that dude, proceed to the nearest exit immediately

26. If you get 'one up' on another man, remember revenge is possible at anytime and anyplace. Keep your head on a swivel. It's coming…

27. No living at home with Mom and Dad beyond the age of 27. You get zero cool points for this living arrangement

28. When waiting at the doctor's office or any establishment with reading material, you must not read women's magazines….no matter how hot the chick is on the cover

29. No beatdowns or any failed manhood challenges shall ever be discussed outside the manhood circle. Yes, you got knocked out, but only we know about it….along with the multitude of witnesses and social media posts. Aside from that, you're good

Women
Articles 30-52

30. Never put your hands on a woman in anger, but dirty looks and talking behind her back is 100% acceptable and expected. Ass slapping or pulling of the hair is permitted if done on request

31. "No" means no. "Not yet" means no. "Wait" means no. A drunk "Yes" means no. Failure to adhere to any of the above will result in a 300-lb cellmate named Bubba whispering sweet nothings in your ear for the next 15 to 20 years

32. Thou shall not flirt with a friend or family member's woman. You are literally begging for a beat-down if you do. Also, keep in mind, she will talk. She is a woman. She must

33. If you EVER get forced into viewing a chick flick, you MUST never disclose that you did so publicly and all evidence must be properly destroyed immediately

34. Bros before chicks (trying to be politically correct), until/unless you haven't had any in 63-days, 9-hrs, 5-minutes and 14-seconds

35. When seated with a woman at a restaurant, the man should never have his back facing the door, unless the woman is bigger, stronger and can fight better than you

36. Never enter another man's domain when his wife or girl is there but he isn't. There will be tension in the room if you do

37. Never let a woman pump gas unless she can out-bench-press you. In that case, sit quietly in the passenger seat and pretend like you are sleep

38. If you absolutely need to be on-time, tell her the show starts at 8:00 when it actually starts at 9:00. Yeah, she'll be a little upset when she finds out, but you'll be on time. Mission accomplished

39. Do not cross swords. Enough said

40. No 'honey dos' during game time – PERIOD. You will be tested often. Stay strong

41. If one of your guy friends accidently sees your wife naked, he must die or be exiled to another country for a minimum of 15-years (unless you are about that life)

42. Never date or attempt to pursue a friend's ex. You may receive a beat-down of epic proportions if you do

43. Attempting to date or otherwise flirt with a friend's mother or sister is strictly prohibited. Cousins can be voted on by the review board

44. If she insists that you hold her purse, you MUST hold it like a football… never by the handle, and you must maintain a look of disgust during the process

45. NOTHING (we repeat NOTHING) your wife or girlfriend wears makes her look fat. Consider yourself warned

46. Happy wife = Happy life. Treat her like a queen always, even when she doesn't act like one. This will ensure your 'night out with the fellas' pass remains valid and accessible

47. If two or more males arrive at a club/ party/social gathering by a single car, and the driving male (under the provisions of article 34) hooks-up with a female, it is the responsibility of the non-driving males to find another way home

48. When your friend picks up a hot girl, however, the hot girl has an ugly friend, it is your official duty to operate as the wing man. As men we are expected to sacrifice and take one for the team knowing that the favor will be repaid

49. No cockblocking – PERIOD. Any such attempt will result in the title 'MITCH' for life

50. No man shall bring a woman to fella's night out. If you are that whipped, stay home

51. Under no circumstances shall a man render control of the television remote to a woman

52. Women who claim to love watching sports must be treated as spies until they demonstrate manlike knowledge of the game. Even then, treat them with suspicion

Children
Articles 53-56

53. Your #1 goal is to keep your daughter off the pole. Just keep repeating, "No clear heels for (insert daughter's name here)"

54. Your #2 goal is to pass-on your sports knowledge, prowess and loyalty to your kids. It's not cool having your sons (especially) wearing enemy colors

55. Never put your hands on a child in anger, but threats like "I brought you in this world and I will take you out" are critically important to the upbringing of a child

56. You are not perfect but do everything in your power to be the kind of man your sons want to emulate and your daughters want to marry. If you don't know how, ask your wife. She will explain everything you are doing wrong

Friendship
Articles 57-71

57. Always correct your friend or brother privately, but NEVER snitch. Snitches get stitches

58. Friends are to be loyal in both good times and bad. Now if times get too tough, proceed to your local barbershop for advice

59. Never turn your back on a friend. If you do, you might get smacked upside the head

60. Honor your word. Do what you said you would do. "I don't remember…" is not an acceptable excuse

61. Never dog-out your friend to a woman. To be clear, it is totally acceptable and expected for men to insult each other. Don't be a MITCH

62. A friend must be allowed to borrow anything you have within 24-hr notice. This law is not applicable to women

63. The maximum amount of time you have to wait for a male friend is 5-minutes. For a woman, you are required to wait at least 15-minutes for every degree of hotness on the 1-10 point scale

64. Always pay your fair share or return the favor as soon as possible. Failure to do so will result in an ugly nickname such as: Cheap-ass Chuck; Mooching-ass Mike; Stingy-ass Stephan; Weasel-ass Wayne….none of which you'll be aware of

65. Bros before chicks, until/unless you haven't had any in 63 days, 9-hrs, 5-minutes and 14-seconds (AKA Man Law #34)

66. When entrusted with another man's secret, take it to your grave. If they happen to dig you up, the proper response will be, "I have no idea"

67. When another man is paying, don't
be greedy. Remember, what goes
around comes around

68. Never leave another man behind in combat, unless he is an asshole and needs to take one for the team

69. Do not allow a man to drive drunk. However, it is perfectly fine to allow him to make an ass out of himself… just for a little while. Chances are he won't remember it anyway

70. Do not lie or cheat your friends. You will never-ever live it down if you do

71. Going Dutch on a hotel room is fine but sharing a bed with another man is strictly prohibited, up to and including head to toe. If there is only one bed, one of you must sleep on the floor. Seniority rules apply here

Attire
Articles 72-89

72. No skinny jeans beyond the age of 20. Absolutely no exceptions! No matter what she says, you look ridiculous. Proceed to the nearest 'grown man' clothing store and get you some gear that actually fits

73. All pants MUST BE properly worn…. no butt cleavage or underwear showing. PULL YOUR DAMN PANTS UP!

74. Long sleeve shirts and jackets must never be tied around your shoulders or waist, unless your flag football belt is broken and it's the only way to tuck your flag

75. Sports jerseys and sweaters should not UNDER ANY CIRCUMSTANCES be tucked inside your pants. For god sakes man….

76. No wearing woman's clothing items EVER. If she insists, don't fall for it. Women talk, and if it gets out on the internet, your life will be over

77. No tight shirts. If man nipples can be seen through your shirt, you are in violation of Man Law

78. When tying shoes, you cannot bend down within 3 feet of another man, and your mouth must remain closed

79. No man should ever in life get a lower back tattoo. No matter what image you choose, nothing will ever be man enough to justify it

80. Every man should own at least 1 dress suit and a pair of nice shoes. It is only a matter of time before you are forced to attend one of those events. Do it to keep the peace and outshine your brother in-law

81. Thou shall not wear socks and sandals. Remember how horrified you were when your grandfather did it?

82. Wearing long socks and shorts is a no no. Don't even think about it

83. No Velcro shoes unless you are a vet 60-years of age or older. Even then, you must have military ID

84. Short shorts and tighty-whities have been officially outlawed. Grown man underwear only; i.e. boxers or boxer briefs. We must evolve

85. No man shall ever pop his shirt collars. Collars are to remain down at all times, unless tying a necktie or mocking a Man Law violator

86. A man purse is still a purse

87. No man shall ever share an umbrella with another man. One or both of you will have to get wet. Seniority rules apply here also

88. Do not attempt or request to borrow clothing items from another man, especially anything worn below the waist. Men's body parts should never occupy the same material or space

89. Do not wash your clothes with another man's laundry. Same rule applies as article 88

Public Facilities
Articles 90-100

90. When using a public shower, there is to be no eyeballing below the shoulders. Also, no eye-to-eye contact for more than 1.5 seconds

91. When entering an empty multi-urinal facility, always proceed to the furthest station to the left or right. Never stand side by side next to another man at the urinal unless ABSOLUTELY POSTIVELY necessary and you must secure at least 2 signatures from men who can vouch for your manhood. Buffering must be maintained or the empire is doomed

92. Eyes forward at the urinal. No eyeballing to the left or right unless you are alone. Even then, it should be kept to a minimum

93. All pee should be properly dispensed
inside the urinal NOT on the floor –
nasty asses

94. The proper woman to man pee ratio is 5 to 1. If you pee with greater frequency, have your bladder checked and/or drastically reduce your alcohol intact

95. Never pee sitting down unless
accompanied by number 2

96. When urinating outside, it is the urinators responsibility to stand at least 10-yards away (preferably near a tree or bush), take a complete 180 degree/full back turn away from the nearest man. No one should see or hear your stream

97. For those standing outside while the urinator (referenced in article 96) is paying the water bill, there is to be no eyeballing of his process. There is to be no conversation with the urinator. His actions are to be completely ignored

98. If you request to use another man's crapper, a quorum must be reached to authorize usage. If a quorum cannot be reached, then you will be SOL – literally and must go elsewhere to handle your situation

99. When using another man's crapper (having met the provisions of article 98), you are required to courtesy flush. Others will soon follow, especially if food is being served

100. It's okay to leave the seat up if it's just guys, but always wipe the rim. Don't be nasty

Food and Beverages
Articles 101-118

101. Grilling season is 24/7/365 and "should" occur in every available weather condition at least once in your lifetime; i.e. rain; sleet; snow, etc.

102. By age 35, you MUST own and/or regularly operate a grill. Charcoal grills are preferred, but gas/propane may be used if authorized by at least 2 of your male counterparts

103. When attending a BBQ, the man working the grill is the closest thing to a king and MUST be addressed as such. 'I will like my steak medium-well your highness'

104. Never put your hands inside another man's potato chip bag, popcorn box or any food packaging apparatus. Toilet paper is not full proof and you know you don't wash your hands as well as you should

105. No gum popping. You look and
sound real stupid

106. When sharing a bottle, alcohol consumption must be as evenly distributed as possible. Any egregious rules violation will result in fines up to and including paying for the next round

107. No backwash. Nobody wants to taste
your spit

108. Unless he has the official title of 'master chef' never ask another man to fix you a plate. Have your lady do it or fix it yourself

109. Never under any circumstances request food from another man's plate. Just embrace it when your woman does it to you. It's in her DNA

110. Unless paralyzed, do not feed or allow another man to feed you with his hands or utensils. Bro don't do it

111. Finger foods such as wings, ribs and pizza should be eaten with your fingers only…never with a knife and fork. Why do you think they call it finger food?

112. When using a straw, it must enter and exit via the east or west corners of your mouth only. North-south entry/exit must be avoided at all costs. Practice at home if necessary

113. Thou shall not lick an ice-cream cone
or suck on a popsicle in public. Aw
hell naw

114. The proper way to eat a banana: you must peel and either break it off piece by piece or use a utensil. Under no circumstances are you to peel and eat whole

115. Always offer the last portion to the woman or your elders. Trust – you will regret it if you don't

116. Do not consume the last of the beer
and take the last chicken wing. It is
one or the other. Greedy ass

117. Never consume fruity alcoholic beverages (AKA bitch-in-a-glass) unless they completely run out of all other forms of 'manly' alcohol. In those scenarios, the beverage must be consumed using a dirty glass

118. When consuming a beverage of any kind, your pinky finger must never be extended. Pinky contact must be maintained with the cup or glass at all times

Barbershop Etiquette
Articles 119-128

Barbers

119. When cutting hair, your package MUST always remain at least 6-inches away from your male customers. No pole to hand or arm contact

120. You MUST thoroughly wash your hands, use hand sanitizer and hand lotion especially after taking a dump. No one wants to smell the remnant on your fingers

121. Stay up on Hot Topics, especially sports. This is the one place where men are expected to socialize and have an opinion

Customers

122. Know your cut and how to explain it. This ain't the hair salon. Chair time is precious and we don't have all day

123. Shower and shampoo prior to arrival. You don't want to smell anything foul coming from your barber and he doesn't want to smell anything foul coming from you

124. Be social without moving your head…
that is, if you care about your edge-up.
Talking with your hands is fine

125. Check your attitude at the door. The barbershop is an escape zone…the place men go to unwind and have pleasant conversation. If you want to waddle in negativity, step outside and call your girlfriend or wife

126. There is always one barber with an empty chair for a prolonged period of time. Beware, he is either the new guy, smells funny or gives horrible shape-ups

127. When/if your hairline reaches 7-inches above your eyebrows, it's time to let it go

128. Tip your barber well. Any advice you need can be found at the barbershop. The average barber, unless he is a neophyte, is part Counselor, Attorney, Politician, Doctor, Sports Analyst, Reporter, Fashion Consultant, Relationship Specialist, Mechanic, etc.

Man Cave Etiquette
Articles 129-132

129. Upon crossing the threshold of another man's man cave, you are now under his jurisdiction. He is your leader. You must submit and adhere to his bylaws

130. Man cave décor must never include the following items: fuzzy pillows; floral arrangements of any kind; the colors pink, yellow or fuchsia

131. When watching football in your man cave, fully clothed women may not enter without permission unless they are serving you food and/or libations

132. Never touch another man's television remote or sound system unless permission is thoroughly expressed and you know what the hell you are doing. A beatdown may be necessary for violators of this Man Law

Sports and Sports Talk
Articles 133-144

133. If you played organized sports at any
level (pee-wee league; high school;
etc.) you are a sports expert. Operate
in your splendor

134. When participating in sports discussions, know your facts or sit quietly in a corner until spoken to

135. Play to win or don't play at all. Victory is much sweeter when you get your opponent's best effort. It's all about bragging rights

136. Man to man butt slapping, although frowned upon by some, is deemed acceptable under the guidelines and provisions of sports participation. The slapper is granted 3 butt slaps per game and only 1 per person

137. Arguments about your favorite sports teams/heroes must never be conceded, they are simply 'to be continued'

138. You MUST be able to name at least half of your favorite team's starters to participate in a sports debate. Failure to do so (if challenged) will render your entire conversation null and void

139. To qualify as a TRUE FAN of any sports team, you MUST have either lived in that city or metropolitan area for at least 5-years; attended a minimum of 2 home games at their stadium/sports arena and/or inherited your sports loyalty from your father. Otherwise, you will be labeled a 'bandwagon fan' and have zero credibility

140. All sports injuries are treatable by walking it off. Lead by example. Limp your ass off the court

141. When participating in sports, there is to be no two-hand touch below the waist. On second thought, no one-hand touch either (excluding article 136)

142. Sports analogies can be used in any conversation to prove any point. Sports is truth

143. No 'honey dos' during game time, PERIOD. You will be tested often. Stay strong (same as article 40)

144. When attending a 'live' sporting event, you MUST represent your favorite team even if your team is not playing. Be prepared to defend your team loyalty. There will be plenty of dirty looks

Road Trip Etiquette

Articles 145-150

145. All male passengers shall pitch in for gas money on all trips over 50 miles, unless you are doing the driver a favor by tagging along. Then the driver should offer you lunch or something

146. Riding shotgun can either be determined by seniority, height/weight, or person who will be most beneficial to the driver. Regardless of who called shotgun, the owner of the vehicle or driver has the final say

147. If you are the navigator, you must
always maintain bass in your voice
and call out all exits/turns in clear and
timely fashion. No vague pointing

148. DO NOT TOUCH the owner's radio! All passengers shall defer to the driver's choice of music. If his taste in music sucks, you'll just have to deal with it. Keep this in mind before deciding who drives

149. When/if the vehicle is full, the youngest and/or most vertically challenged occupant must sit in the middle back seat (AKA "riding bitch")

150. You MUST take advantage of all restroom opportunities, even if you don't really have to go, to avoid additional stops. Otherwise, you MUST pee sitting down for the remainder of the trip

Weed Smoking Etiquette

(must be included although the author does not support or advocate this behavior)

Articles 151-155

151. Respect rolling protocol. You should know how your joint rolling skills stack up against your counterparts. The most experienced roller does the rolling

152. He who did the rolling shall light

153. It's puff-puff pass, puff-puff pass.
Don't hog the joint

154. Stick to the original rotation. Typically, the roller will light, take two puffs and pass counter-clockwise

155. Keep your exhale to yourself. No one likes taking a cloud in the grill

Violation of any of the aforementioned Man Laws must be met with serious consequences including: severe clowning; hateful stares; public ridicule; outing on social media; and confiscating of the Man Card if the council deems necessary

Definition of Terms

Bitch in a Glass
: Fruity alcoholic beverages, which are regularly consumed by women

Cockblocking
: One guy ruining another guy's chance to score with a female

Cross Swords
: When two or more guys are having sex with a female and they accidently touch penises; much like two swords dueling

Grown Man
: A mature adult male that handles his business

Hole
: Anus, Buttocks or butt

Honey Dos
: A list of chores assigned by one's primary companion or sweetheart

Man Cave
: A room, space, corner or area of a dwelling that is specifically reserved for a male person to be in a solitary condition, away from the rest of the household to work, play, involve himself in certain hobbies, activities without interruption. This area is usually decorated by the male that uses it without interference from any female influence

Mitch
: A male version of a bitch. (According to Kevin Hart in Real Husbands of Hollywood)

Paying Water Bill
: 'Nickname' used to describe the process of urinating

Pole	Penis. Body part found on males used to urinate and pleasure
Shotgun	Sitting in the front passenger seat of a vehicle
SSS	Three S's – Shit, Shower, Shave
Riding Bitch	Riding in the middle back seat of a vehicle
Rolling	Process used to roll a joint
Weed	Marijuana

www.ingramcontent.com/pod-product-compliance
Lightning Source LLC
Chambersburg PA
CBHW060545160726
47991CB00001B/445